Chicago

by Jessica Rudolph

Consultant: Karla Ruiz, MA
Teachers College, Columbia University
New York, New York

New York, New York

Credits

Cover, © Ian Dagnall/Alamy Stock Photo; 2, © Songquan Deng/Shutterstock; TOC, © Keith Levit/Shutterstock; 4–5, © Richard Cavalleri/Shutterstock; 7, © AnLuNi/Shutterstock; 8–9, © Ryszard_Kania/iStock; 10, © Nippon News/Alamy Stock Photo; 11T, © Merle Laswell/Icon Sportswire DHF/Newscom; 11B, © Tribune Content Agency LLC/Alamy Stock Photo; 12, © Rudy Balasko/Shutterstock; 13, © Kubrak78/iStock; 14, © Maria Burmistrova/Shutterstock; 15, © Brent Hofacker/Shutterstock; 16–17, © Fotoluminate LLC/Shutterstock; 18, © Travel Pictures/Alamy Stock Photo; 19, © Erdal Bayhan/Dreamstime; 20, © Richard Ellis/Alamy Stock Photo; 20–21, © Starcevic/iStock; 22 (Clockwise from Top Right), © haveseen/Shutterstock, © Richard Cavalleri/Shutterstock, © Rudy Balasko/Shutterstock, and © stevegeer/iStock; 23 (T to B), © Thomas Barrat/Shutterstock, © Erdal Bayhan/Dreamstime, © Ryszard_Kania/iStock, © shinyshot/Shutterstock, and © Suzanne Tucker/Shutterstock; 24, © Richard Cavalleri/Shutterstock.

Publisher: Kenn Goin
Editor: J. Clark
Creative Director: Spencer Brinker
Photo Researcher: Thomas Persano

Library of Congress Cataloging-in-Publication Data
Names: Rudolph, Jessica, author.
Title: Chicago / by Jessica Rudolph.
Description: New York, New York : Bearport Publishing, 2018. | Series: Citified! | Includes bibliographical references and index. | Audience: Ages 5–8.
Identifiers: LCCN 2017005330 (print) | LCCN 2017006261 (ebook) | ISBN 9781684022342 (library) | ISBN 9781684022885 (ebook)
Subjects: LCSH: Chicago (Ill.)—Juvenile literature.
Classification: LCC F548.33 .R83 2018 (print) | LCC F548.33 (ebook) | DDC 977.3/11—dc23
LC record available at https://lccn.loc.gov/2017005330

Copyright © 2018 Bearport Publishing Company, Inc. All rights reserved. No part of this publication may be reproduced in whole or in part, stored in any retrieval system, or transmitted in any form or by any means, electronic, mechanical, photocopying, recording, or otherwise, without written permission from the publisher.

For more information, write to Bearport Publishing Company, Inc., 45 West 21st Street, Suite 3B, New York, New York 10010. Printed in the United States of America.

10 9 8 7 6 5 4 3 2 1

Contents

Chicago 4

Map It! 22

Glossary 23

Index 24

Read More 24

Learn More Online 24

About the Author 24

Chicago is in Illinois.

It's the third-largest city in the United States.

Nearly three million people live there!

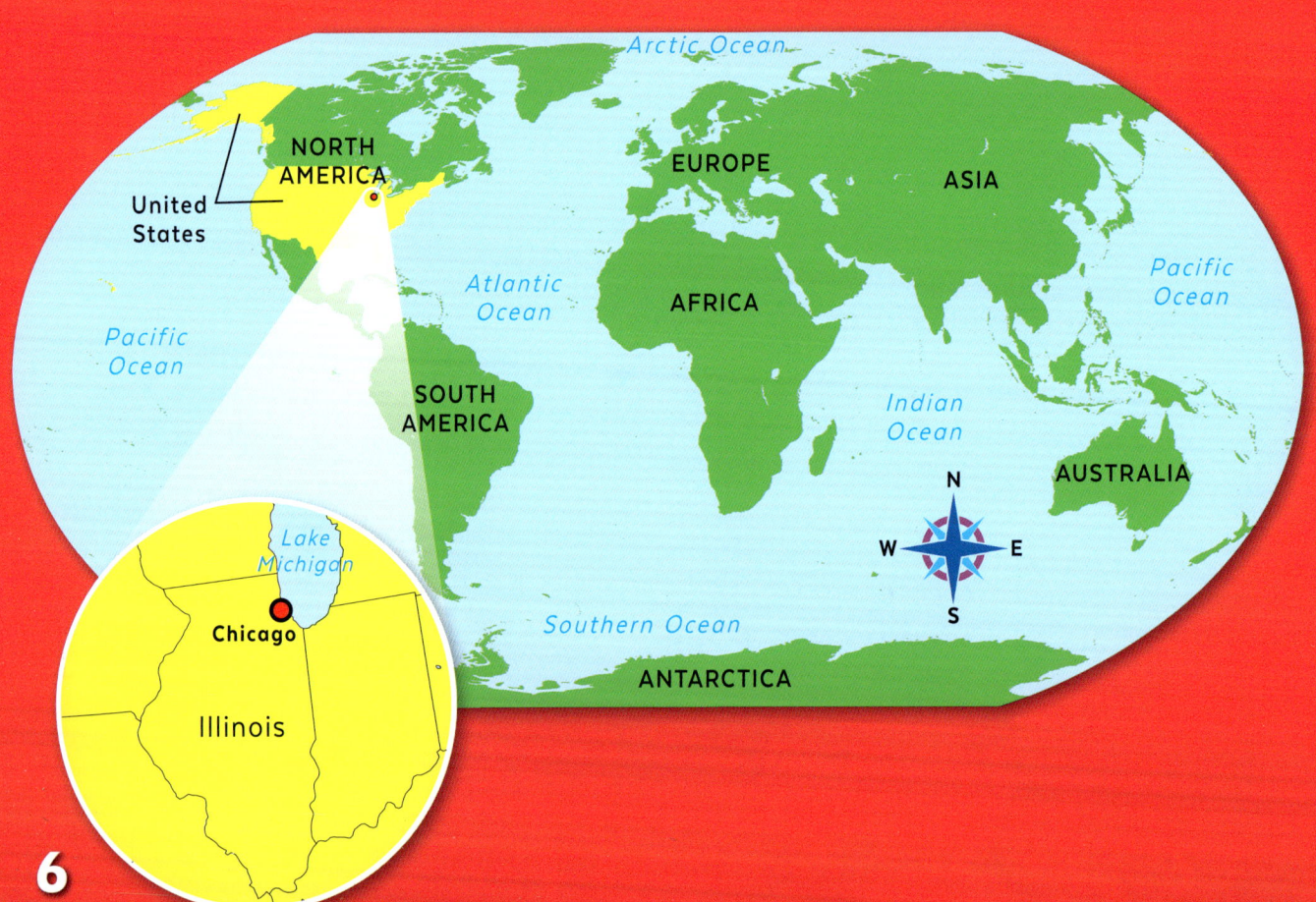

Chicago lies along Lake Michigan, which is one of the five Great Lakes.

Brrr! Chicago is known for its **frigid** winters.

In the coldest months, part of Lake Michigan freezes over.

The coldest recorded temperature in Chicago was -27°F (-33°C)! That was on January 20, 1985.

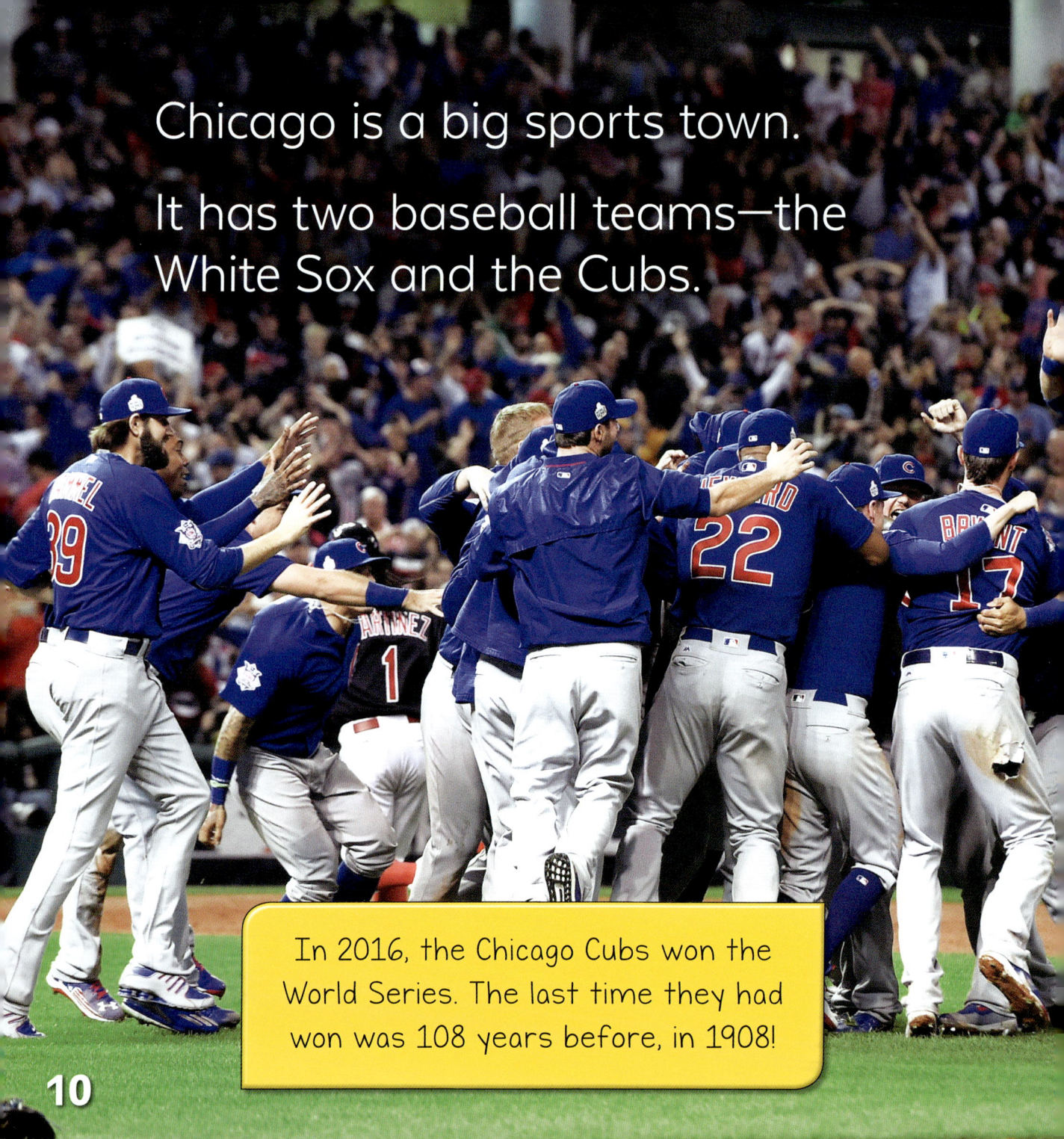

Chicago is a big sports town.

It has two baseball teams—the White Sox and the Cubs.

In 2016, the Chicago Cubs won the World Series. The last time they had won was 108 years before, in 1908!

Fans root for their football team, the Bears.

They cheer for the basketball team, the Bulls.

The best views of the city are seen from the Willis Tower.

This is the tallest building in Chicago.

It soars 1,450 feet (442 m)!

If you don't have a fear of heights, step onto the Ledge. You can look through the glass floor 1,353 feet (412 m) below!

Chicago has great food.

Hot dogs are very popular.

Most people top them with pickles, peppers, and onions.

Chicago-style hot dogs are slathered with mustard, but not ketchup!

Chicago is where deep-dish pizza was **invented**. This style of pizza has a thick crust.

Where's a great place to relax in Chicago?

Go to Millennium Park.

On a hot day, cool off at the fountain.

Chicago has more than 500 parks!

You can hear lots of great music in the city.

Try a blues club!

Every year, the city holds a blues **festival**.

The Chicago River flows through the city.

Tourists can zoom around on tour boats.

Guides on the boats point out major sights along the river.

kayak

Many people like to get exercise by paddling kayaks down the Chicago River.

Chicago

Lake Michigan

Millennium Park

Chicago River

Willis Tower

Cool Fact: To celebrate St. Patrick's Day, the city **dyes** the Chicago River green!

dyes (DYEZ) colors or stains something

festival (FESS-tih-vuhl) a regularly occurring program of activities or entertainment

frigid (FRIJ-id) freezing cold

invented (in-VEN-tid) first created

tourists (TOOR-ists) people who travel to and visit places for pleasure

Index

blues 18–19
Chicago River 20–21, 22
food 14–15
Lake Michigan 7, 8–9, 22
Millennium Park 16–17, 22
sports 10–11
Willis Tower 12–13, 22
winter 8–9

Read More

Bartlett, Karen T. *A Kid's Guide to Chicago.* Rockport, MA: Twin Lights Publishers (2010).

Hurd, Owen. *Chicago History for Kids: Triumphs and Tragedies of the Windy City.* Chicago: Chicago Review Press (2007).

Learn More Online

To learn more about Chicago, visit
www.bearportpublishing.com/Citified

About the Author

Jessica Rudolph has written many books about history, science, and nature for children. She thinks Chicago-style deep dish is the best kind of pizza.